■ SCHOLASTIC

Hands-On History

PIONEERS

by Michael Gravois

WITHDRAWN

New York • Toronto • London • Auckland • Sydney
Mexico City • New Delhi • Hong Kong • Buenos Aires

Teaching Resources

Dedication

To my brother, Wade Gravois,
who has the spirit of a pioneer
and the soul of a frontiersman

Scholastic Inc. grants teachers permission to photocopy the designated reproducible pages for classroom use.
No other part of this publication may be reproduced in whole or in part, or stored in a retrieval system,
or transmitted in any form or by any means, electronic, mechanical, photocopying, recording,
or otherwise, without written permission of the publisher.
For information regarding permission, write to Scholastic Inc., 557 Broadway, New York, NY 10012.

Cover design by Jason Robinson
Interior design by Michael Gravois
Interior illustrations by Jim Palmer
Photo Acknowledgements
The photographs are reproduced with the permission of:
© California State Library, Neg #911, p. 22

ISBN 0-439-41126-2

Copyright © 2004 by Michael Gravois. All rights reserved.

Printed in the U.S.A.

1 2 3 4 5 6 7 8 9 10   40   11 10 09 08 07 06 05 04

Table of Contents

Introduction

As a middle-school teacher, I was always looking for ways to keep students interested and enthusiastic about learning. I developed activities and projects that helped me teach the required curriculum and also made my lessons fun, hands-on, diverse, and challenging.

I used an interactive-project approach with my fifth-grade students, and I can't stress enough how much they enjoyed it. Throughout each unit I had my students keep the activity sheets and projects in a pocket folder, so they could assemble a student-made textbook on the subject we were studying. They used these textbooks as a study guide for the final test. I was amazed at the higher-level thinking that took place in class discussions and by the degree of knowledge the students had acquired by the end of each unit. Parents even commented on the unique way the information was presented and how easy it was for their children to study for the final test. After seeing my students' success, I decided to put my ideas on paper. *Hands-On History: Pioneers* is a compilation of the activities I used to teach about pioneers.

For each activity and project, I've included detailed instructions. Many of the activities incorporate language arts and critical thinking skills such as differentiating fact and opinion, comparing and contrasting, the 5 Ws (who, what, where, when, why), understanding cause and effect, writing a letter, brainstorming, and sequencing.

I hope your students enjoy these projects as much as mine did.

How to Use This Book

Supplies

At the beginning of the school year, ask students to bring in the materials needed to create projects throughout the year. Also arrange the classroom desks into clusters, each with a bin to hold pens, markers, gluesticks, scissors, and other needed supplies. This enables students to share the materials. You should have each of your students bring in the following supplies:
- a roll of tape
- several glue sticks
- a good pair of scissors
- a packet of colored pencils
- a packet of thin, colored markers
- a project folder (pocket-type) to hold papers and other materials related to the projects

Maximizing Learning

Because students have different learning styles, you may first want to orally summarize the information you will be covering that day. Then you can read the related section in the textbook or trade book. Finally, have students complete the activity. This not only exposes visual, aural, and artistic learners to the information through their strongest learning style, but it also allows them to review the same information several times.

Brainstorming About Pioneers

Materials: copies of pages 28–31, chart paper, markers

After introducing the concept of pioneers and the Westward Movement, conduct the following activity. It offers a hands-on way for students to brainstorm and discuss aspects of the Westward Movement and provides the materials for an educational display in the classroom or hall.

1. Have students work in groups of four.

2. Copy the four question sheets on pages 28–31 and give each student in the group a different question sheet.

3. Pair up two groups and have the members of both groups arrange their four chairs so that they are sitting in a line facing one another.

4. When you say, "BEGIN," students in Group 1 read their question to the person in Group 2 whom they are facing. Instruct the respondee to answer the question while the questioner records the answer on the question sheet. Allow two to three minutes for this, and then tell students to stop.

5. When you say, "BEGIN," students in Group 2 read their question to the person in Group 1 whom they are facing and record the answers on the question sheet. Allow two to three minutes for this, and then tell students to stop.

6. When you say, "SWITCH," the members of Group 1 rotate—the first person goes to the last seat, and the other three members move over one seat. They will now be facing new members in Group 2 (Group 2 does not move at all).

7. Repeat steps 4, 5, and 6 until each member in Group 1 has asked his or her question of each member in Group 2, and has responded to each question from Group 2. At one point each student will respond to the same question that he or she has asked.

8. Have students who asked Question A meet with one another and record on chart paper all of the answers that were gathered (the question should be pre-written at the top of the chart paper). Tell students to record only appropriate responses. Students who asked Questions B, C, and D should also meet in groups and record appropriate responses.

9. After students have recorded the answers, ask one student from each group to read them. Discuss the answers as a class and add any information you feel should have been included. (Some possible answers to each of the questions can be found on page 6.)

10. Hang these questions and answers in the classroom so that students can refer to them throughout this unit.

Suggested Answers to Questions

QUESTION A: What are some of the reasons pioneers decided to move west?

REASONS: Manifest Destiny, wealth, to find gold, to escape slavery, to claim land of their own, farming, curiosity, hunting and trapping, religious freedom, overcrowding in the East, to bring Christianity to the Indians

QUESTION B: What were some of the difficulties and dangers the pioneers faced before and during their journey?

DIFFICULTIES AND DANGERS: Leaving loved ones behind, finding water and food along the trail, bad weather, hostile Indians, sickness, wild animals, rough terrain (mountains, rivers, forests, etc.), boredom, getting lost, broken wagon wheels

QUESTION C: What methods of transportation did pioneers use? What differences would they find in today's world?

PIONEER TRANSPORTATION: Wagon trains, Conestoga wagons, flat-bottomed boats, horses, ships (around South America), stagecoach, mule barge, steamboat

MODERN TRANSPORTATION: Paved roads and highways, cars, planes, trains. It took pioneers months to cross the country, but we can now do it in hours on an airplane. There are places to eat and rest all across the country today.

QUESTION D: What qualities would a pioneer have to possess?

QUALITIES: Bravery, curiosity, intelligence, map-reading skills, marksmanship, strength, health, desire

Pioneering Vocabulary Bulletin Board

Materials: copies of page 32, colored markers or pencils, scissors, stapler

At the beginning of the Pioneers unit, set up a "Pioneering Vocabulary" bulletin board that students can add to as the unit unfolds.

CREATING THE BULLETIN BOARD

1. Create a background of mountains and add a title banner that reads "Pioneering Vocabulary."
2. Have students take turns writing each new vocabulary word on the wagon template and its definition as they learn it.
3. Then have students color the wagon and add it to the wagon train on the bulletin board.
4. Keep a supply of "vocabulary wagons" handy for students to use. See the list on page 7 for possible words and their definitions.

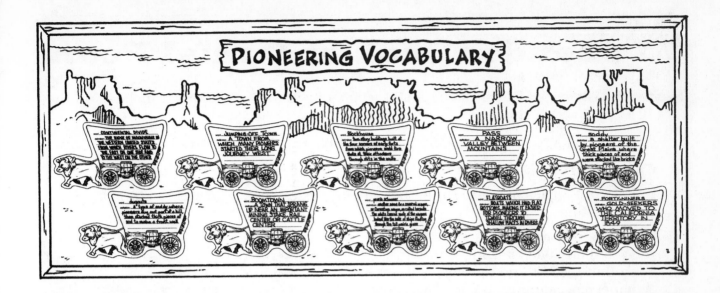

Word List

blockhouse: two-story building built at each corner of early forts from which pioneers could fire shots at their attackers through slits in the walls

boomtown: a town that sprang up near an important mining stake, rail center, or cattle center

cholera: a common and deadly disease that pioneers caught by drinking dirty water

Continental Divide: the ridge of mountains in the western United States from which rivers flow to the east on one side and to the west on the other

dugout: a type of soddy where pioneers dug out part of a hill, then stacked thick pieces of sod to make a front wall (see *soddy*)

flatboats: boats that had flat bottoms, making it easier for pioneers to travel through shallow places in rivers

forty-niners: gold seekers who moved to the California Territory in 1849

jumping-off town: a town from which many pioneers started their long journey west

Manifest Destiny: a phrase used by leaders and politicians in the 1840s explaining that continental expansion by the United States was a "mission" or national destiny

pass: a narrow valley between mountains

pioneer: one of the first people to settle in a place

prairie schooner: another name for a covered wagon, or Conestoga wagon, so called because the white canvas roofs of the wagons looked like the sails of ships floating through the tall prairie grass

soddy: a shelter built by pioneers of the Great Plains with thick pieces of sod stacked like bricks

Meander Book of Daniel Boone

Materials: copies of pages 33 and 34 (copied back-to-back so that panel 1 is on the side directly behind the cover), scissors

Have students read about Daniel Boone and his exploits in Kentucky.

CREATING THE MEANDER BOOK

1. Pass out copies of the meander book template and ask students to cut along the dotted lines.

2. Have students fold the meander books accordion-style (starting with panel 1), so that the left and right sides of each panel close onto each other like a book (i.e., first fold panel 1 in half, turn the paper over and fold panel 2 in half, turn the paper over and fold panel 3 in half, and continue folding until all eight panels are closed).

3. Students will "meander" their way through the book in order to complete the eight panels.

Possible Answers for Meander Book Questions

PANEL 1: Reasons why people wanted to settle the land in Kentucky: overcrowding on the East Coast, fertile land for farming, land could be bought cheaply, adventure

Reasons that made their journey to this area difficult: mountains, American Indians, loneliness, getting lost, far from cities and supplies

PANEL 2: Daniel Boone answered this way because he felt at home in the woods. Therefore, he never felt lost—even if he wasn't sure of the way to get home. He knew he would find his way at some point.

PANEL 3: The Cumberland Gap is in Kentucky. It was important because it provided a way for the pioneers to get between the mountains instead of having to go over them.

PANEL 4: Blockhouses are two-story buildings built at the four corners of early forts from which pioneers could fire shots at their attackers through slits in the walls.

PANEL 5: The state flower is the goldenrod, the state tree is the tulip tree, and the state bird is the Kentucky cardinal.

PANEL 6: Nouns that could describe Boone are *hunter, explorer, fighter, trailblazer, pathfinder, frontiersman*.

PANEL 7: Adjectives that could describe Boone are *brave, adventurous, knowledgeable, independent, inquisitive, determined*.

PANEL 8: Accept all reasonable responses.

Louisiana Purchase Map and Pop-Up Monuments

Materials: copies of pages 35 and 36,
scissors, legal-size copier paper (8½" by 14"),
glue sticks, colored markers or pencils

Give students copies of the Louisiana Purchase map
on page 35. Have them follow the directions on the
template to complete their keys and maps. They
should cut out the completed maps—which will be
used as the cover of the pop-up books they will
create—and put them in their project folders.

Give students sheets of legal-size copier paper. Have
them follow the directions below to make the pop-up
monuments page.

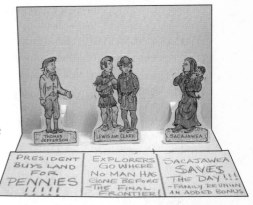

CREATING THE POP-UP MONUMENTS

1. Have students place
   the copier paper in
   horizontally, then
   measure 5½" from
   the left and fold.

2. Ask students to measure
   3" from the right and fold.
   Then they should tuck this
   panel behind the first fold.

3. Have students place a small pencil
   mark along the first folded edge at
   the following six measurements: 1",
   2", 3¾", 4¾", 6½",
   and 7½". Then they
   should cut a 1¼" slit
   along the folded edge
   at each mark.

4. Instruct students to open the paper
   and gently pull each pop-up tab for-
   ward. Then have them fold the
   paper again so that
   each pop-up tab falls
   into the center. They
   should make a
   crease at the base of
   each tab.

5. Ask students to color the monuments of Jefferson, Lewis and Clark,
   and Sacajawea on page 36. Then
   have them cut out the figures, and
   glue them to the tabs.

6. Have students divide the long
   horizontal panel underneath the
   monuments into three sections.
   Then ask them to write a
   sensational headline that describes
   the role each figure played in the
   acquisition and exploration of the
   Louisiana Territory.

7. Instruct students to open up the
   long horizontal strip, then divide
   this area underneath the monuments into three vertical sections,
   and write a news
   article that describes
   the importance of
   each figure's
   involvement with the
   Louisiana Territory.

8. Using a glue stick, students should
   then glue the map of the Louisiana
   Purchase to
   the cover of
   the pop-up
   book.

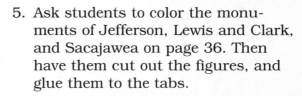

put glue here

Trail of Tears Story Scroll

Materials: copies of page 37, brown paper bags, yarn,
masking tape, markers, poster paint, scissors,
hole punch, thin wooden dowels (20" long)

In this cooperative activity, students will learn about
the reaction of Native Americans to the stream of settlers coming to their lands and how they were treated
by the United States government.

CONDUCTING THE COOPERATIVE ACTIVITY

1. Break the class up into groups of three. Each person in the group will become an
   expert in one of three subjects: Tecumseh, the Indian Removal Act, or the Trail of
   Tears. (You can have larger groups with more students and more
   subjects, such as Sequoyah, the Osceola tribe, the Black Hawk War, the Cherokee
   Nation, and so on.)

2. Next, have the experts in each subject meet with each other, research their topic,
   and write down all of the important facts that they want to include in their story. At
   this point, you might meet with each group to check on the facts they've chosen and
   add information they might have neglected to include.

3. Then have each student write a short story
   about the subject they studied. Tell them to use
   vivid adjectives and interesting nouns. Explain
   that they will be creating iconographic stories—
   visual pictures that represent words and ideas—
   similar to the style that many Native American
   groups used to communicate. The icons should
   be simple, invented images with bold strokes
   that represent elements in their story. (See the
   example to the right.) As a historical side note,
   explain that Sequoyah, a Cherokee Indian,
   developed a written language and alphabet for
   the Cherokee people between 1809 and 1821.

TRANSLATION:
*It took over a year for the Cherokee
people to march eight hundred miles
during the Trail of Tears.*

4. Give students copies of the scroll template on page 37 to use when mapping out
   the icons for their story. This will be their rough draft. Then have students complete a finished scroll by following the directions on page 11.

5. Have students return to their original group of three. Make two copies of each student's template so they can give a copy to each of their original groupmates.
   Students will present their finished scroll to their groupmates and read (i.e., trans-
   late) it to them. Groupmates will transcribe the translation on their copy of the template. This allows each student to record all of the necessary information about all
   the subject areas, and they get to practice their speaking and listening skills at the
   same time.

6. Display the scrolls and the translated stories on a bulletin board in the hall.

CREATING THE STORY SCROLL

1. Give students brown grocery bags, and have them cut a 16" by 18" rectangle out of it. They should cut a meandering edge so their bags look like animal hides.

2. Have students use bold black markers to draw the icons for their stories on the scrolls. They could use colored markers or poster paints to add color.

3. Once the paint is dry, students should crumple up the scrolls and then reopen and flatten them out. This adds texture to the "animal hides."

4. On the back of their scrolls, have students add a piece of masking tape to the four corners. Then ask them to use a hole punch to make a hole in the four corners.

5. Instruct students to tie a 12" piece of yarn through each hole.

6. Give each student two 20" dowels. (These can be collected later to be used again next year.) Students should tie the four pieces of yarn to the dowels, fastening one piece to each corner of the scroll, so the scroll looks like a stretched animal hide.

The Westward Movement— Two Points of View

We can learn a lot about our history by looking at the past from different points of view. We can also learn about how history applies to our lives today by looking at events from the perspective of people who lived long ago.

From a modern perspective, the government's treatment of Native Americans was reprehensible. But in the 18th and 19th centuries, most early settlers felt it was their Manifest Destiny to claim land and settle the country from sea to sea. Many felt that the Native Americans were inferior because they didn't hold the same religious beliefs. Overcrowding on the East Coast and the prospect of cheap, fertile farmland in other areas drove the settlers farther and farther westward. Stories of gold on Native American lands spurred the government to remove the tribes from their homes. But most importantly, and perhaps tragically, it was hard for settlers to see the similarities and differences between the Native Americans and themselves.

The same types of problems exist around the world today when two different groups want the same land or when different races clash because of the actions of a few. It is important to look at the big picture from all vantage points. More often than not, we can find many similarities between the groups.

CREATING THE BULLETIN BOARD

1. Lead a discussion about the different points of view between the settlers and the Native Americans.

2. Divide the class into two groups: settlers and Native Americans. Have each student write a letter to the other group explaining why his or her group should have the land. They should design stationery for the published version of their letter by creating a border around their writing that features Native American designs or colonial icons (depending on the perspective they're representing).

3. Divide a bulletin board in half and hang up the opposing viewpoints on opposite sides. Add a banner that reads "The Westward Movement: Differing Perspectives."

Texas Time Line— Settlers Move to Texas

Materials: copies of page 38, scissors, tape

Have your students read about the early pioneers who settled in Texas, the battle of the Alamo, and the admittance of Texas into the Union. Then give each student a copy of the template on page 38.

CREATING THE TEXAS TIME LINE

1. Tell students to cut the sheet in half vertically along the dotted line to make two long strips of paper.

2. Have them tape the strips into one long time line. (Students should tape their time lines from behind so that the tape does not cover the area on which they are going to write.)

3. Demonstrate how to fold this long time line accordion-style so that all of the writing is on the inside. When the time line is closed, the top panel should be blank.

4. On this top panel, ask students to write "[Your name]'s Time Line of Texas," using creative lettering, and to draw an illustration of the Texas state flag under the title.

5. Then have students complete the panels to show their knowledge of the westward expansion into the state of Texas.

Suggested Answers for Time Line Questions

PANEL 1—1821: Before 1821, Texas was part of the Spanish territory of Mexico. Then Mexico won its independence from Spain after years of hard fighting.

PANEL 2—1820s: Mexico wanted to build up the Texas territory by having more people settle there. They allowed *Stephen Austin* to bring 300 families from the United States to settle in Texas. Then more and more Americans started to move there.

Today, the capital of Texas is named Austin in his honor.

PANEL 3—1830: Mexico banned Americans from continuing to settle in Texas because the settlers didn't convert to Catholicism as Mexico wanted; they refused to learn Spanish, which was the national language; many settlers had slaves, which was not allowed in Mexico; the settlers would not become loyal to Mexico rather than to the

United States; American settlers outnumbered Mexican residents by three to one, and Mexico was afraid it would lose control of the territory.

PANELS 4, 5, and 6—1836: *General Antonio López de Santa Anna,* the ruler of Mexico, led his army to the Alamo in order to overpower the Texans who sought independence. *Juan Seguín* was a Tejano leader who organized the men who joined the volunteer Texas Army in the fight for independence. *William Travis,* a lawyer from Alabama, was the 27-year-old commander of the Texas Army who led the fight at the Alamo. *Davy Crockett* was a frontiersman and former U.S. congressman from Tennessee who fought and died at the Alamo. *Jim Bowie,* the inventor of a special hunting knife called the bowie knife, also fought and died at the Alamo. After Santa Anna won the battle at the Alamo, *Sam Houston* led a surprise attack against him at the battle of San Jacinto, which forced Santa Anna to grant Texas its independence from Mexico.

PANEL 7—1845: President Andrew Jackson was afraid that Mexico would declare war if the United States allowed Texas to become a state. Also, Texas allowed slavery, and many northern leaders did not want to let another slave state into the Union.

Westward Ho!—Guidebook for a Difficult Journey

Materials: white copier paper, brown construction paper, colored markers, scissors, glue sticks

Brainstorm a list of difficulties that the pioneers faced on their journey west. You might consider showing select scenes from the movie *How the West Was Won* (such as when the characters face the difficulty of going up a hill or losing a wagon wheel).

Then have students create ten-page books called *A Pioneer's Guidebook for a Difficult Journey* (see page 14 for instructions). Each page should contain a difficulty the pioneers faced, an illustration of that difficulty, and a couple of sentences describing a pioneer should do if confronted by that difficulty.

The list of difficulties that the pioneers faced should include (among others) conflicts with Native Americans, wild animals, bad weather, sickness and death, difficult terrain, leaving loved ones, finding water and food on the trail, boredom, getting lost, or breaking a wagon wheel. Some of these topics can be broken down further; for example, weather can be separated into what to do in the event of snow or in the event of heavy rains—both conditions that presented unique problems for pioneers trying to cross mountains, rivers, or forests.

1. Have students cut two sheets of copy paper in half widthwise. (Since students will use only three of these half pages, have them share.)

2. Instruct students to fold all three sheets in half widthwise and place a small pencil mark on the folded edge 1³⁄₈" from either side.

3. Ask students to open up the pages. Then have them cut a slit in two of the sheets along the folded edge from the outer edges up to the pencil mark (two slits in each sheet).

4. Have students cut a slit in the center of the third page, from one pencil mark to the other.

5. Ask students to place the two identically cut sheets on top of each other. Then they should curl the sides of the sheets into a cylinder and feed them through the hole in the third sheet.

6. Have students open up the sheets so they lock into place, then fold the pages into a book shape.

7. Using a glue stick have students glue a sheet of brown construction paper around the cover. Then they should trim the construction paper so there is a half-inch border around the pages. Have students use creative lettering to title the book *A Pioneer's Guidebook for a Difficult Journey.*

8. Ask students to choose ten difficulties the pioneers could face on their journey and then write the difficulty on each page, draw an illustration of that difficulty, and write a couple of sentences telling the pioneers what to do if they encounter that difficulty on their journey.

Pioneer Trunk

Materials: trade books about the westward movement, colored construction paper, scissors, colored markers or pencils, glue sticks

On the journey west, pioneers didn't ride in their covered wagons (except for old people and babies). Instead, the wagons were used for storage. It was vitally important that the pioneers pack the proper amount of items to ensure a safe trip. Packing too little food and supplies could lead to starvation or being unprepared to start a new life when the journey ended; packing too much could overburden and even kill the animals pulling the wagon. Such a loss of transportation power could slow or stop the journey.

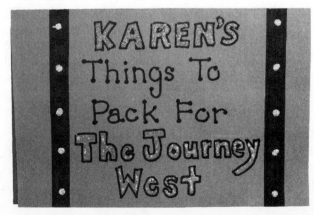

Gather trade books that detail the journey the pioneers took in their quest for a new life. There are many books on this subject available in the library. Some of my favorites are *Daily Life in a Covered Wagon* by Paul Erickson (Puffin Books, 1994), *If You Traveled West in a Covered Wagon* by Ellen Levine (Scholastic, 1992), and *Wagon Wheel Kitchens* by Jacqueline Williams (University Press of Kansas, 1993).

Tell students that they should research different items that pioneers took with them on their journey—the types and amount of food they brought, the clothing they wore or packed, materials needed to keep the wagon in good condition, keepsakes and furniture, and supplies needed to start a new life at the end of their trip. For instance, in *Wagon Wheel Kitchens*, Jacqueline Williams writes that the suggested amount of food for *each adult* in the group included 200 pounds of flour, 30 pounds of pilot bread, 75 pounds of bacon, 10 pounds of rice, 5 pounds of coffee, 2 pounds of tea, 25 pounds of sugar, ½ bushel of dried beans, 1 bushel of dried fruit, 2 pounds of baking soda, 10 pounds of salt, ½ bushel of cornmeal, ½ bushel of corn (parched and ground), and 1 small keg of vinegar.

Explain that students will design a trunk with three "compartments" that contain items (and descriptions of the items) that the pioneers might have taken with them.

CREATING THE TRUNK

1. Give each student one large and three small sheets of construction paper. Students should fold the three smaller sheets in half horizontally. These sheets represent the three compartments of the trunk or wagon. Each compartment should focus on a different category of supplies needed for the journey—food, clothing, tools to fix the wagon, keepsakes, furniture, or materials to start a new life.

2. Ask students to draw and cut out different items related to each of the categories of supplies they've chosen to represent in their trunks. (For example, if the compartment focuses on tools needed to fix the wagon, they might draw a spare wheel, a spare axle, a bucket of grease, and a bucket of tar.) These items should be glued around the inside of the folded piece of construction paper.

3. Next to each item, have students write a description of the item and explain why each it needed.

4. Instruct students to repeat steps 2 and 3 for each compartment.

CONTINUED ON PAGE 16

Pop-Up Trunks

For a more interesting and inventive trunk, have students create pop-up elements in each compartment. You can adapt the instructions for the Pop-Up Monuments on page 9 for this. Have students vary the lengths of the tabs to make the items in the compartments more three-dimensional. Students can "pack" additional items into the compartment by gluing them below and above the pop-up elements.

CREATING THE TRUNK (CONTINUED)

5. When they have finished the three compartments, tell students to glue the bottom of one compartment to the top side of the next, until the three pages are joined and turn like the pages in a book. (Have them use glue sticks instead of regular glue so that the paper doesn't buckle.)

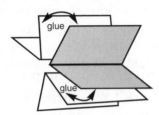

6. Students should fold the large sheet of construction paper over the three compartments, cut it to fit, and then glue it to bind them, creating a cover for the trunk. Brown construction paper works well because it looks more like an old leather trunk.

7. Finally, have students decorate their covers so they look like old trunks, complete with straps, rivets, and lock. They should add their name and a title, such as "Things to Pack for the Journey West."

Mapping the Journey

Materials: copy of page 39, overhead transparency of the map, colored markers

Pioneers could choose from several different trails for their journey west, depending on where they wanted to settle. With this activity, students hone their mapping skills as they trace the different routes the pioneers took more than 150 years ago.

CREATING THE MAP

1. Pass out a copy of the map template on page 39 to each student.

2. Describe the four major trails used by the pioneers as you trace the routes on an overhead transparency using a different color for each trail. Students will use colored markers to trace the routes themselves on their templates, filling in the key with the appropriate color as they follow along.

3. **Tracing the Oregon Trail**—The jumping-off point for the Oregon trail started at Independence, Missouri. Students should place their markers on the dot representing Independence and trace the trail as you describe its path. From Independence, the pioneers headed to Fort Kearny. They then traveled along the North Platte River, passing Chimney Rock, and resting at Fort Laramie. They continued along the river, passing Independence Rock, and heading through the South Pass toward Fort Bridger. From Fort Bridger, they headed north to Fort Hall and traveled along the Snake River to Fort Boise. Their journey almost complete, they headed north to Fort Walla Walla and across the Cascade Range to Portland in the Oregon Territory.

CONTINUED ON PAGE 17

###

CREATING THE MAP *(CONTINUED)*

4. **Tracing the California Trail**—Using a different colored marker, have students trace the California Trail, which branched off from the Oregon Trail shortly after the stop at Fort Hall. It meandered over to the Sierra Nevada Mountains, through the Donner Pass, and ended at Sutter's Fort (which is present-day Sacramento).

5. **Tracing the Santa Fe Trail**—The Santa Fe Trail also began at Independence, Missouri. From there, the pioneers traveled to Fort Dodge, continued on along the Arkansas River to Bent's Fort, ending their journey in Santa Fe.

6. **Tracing the Old Spanish Trail**—The Old Spanish Trail was a continuation of the Santa Fe Trail, with its jumping-off point at Santa Fe. From here, pioneers continued in a northwest direction. Once they crossed the Colorado River they turned southwest, crossed the Mojave Desert and Sierra Madre Mountains, and headed to Los Angeles.

7. After they have traced all four trails, have students fill in the map key with the color that corresponds to each trail. They should keep their maps handy so they can use them for the next activity.

Video Diary of the Trip West

Materials: oak tag or poster board, craft sticks, copies of pages 40–43, scissors, tape, colored markers or pencils, stapler

Today, many families document major journeys and events in their lives using video cameras. Ask your students to imagine the types of things that pioneers might have documented had they taken a video camera on their journey.

CREATING THE VIDEO DIARY

1. Pass out copies of the templates on pages 42 and 43. Using the film strip template, students will create six illustrations that detail major events from the journey of a fictional family traveling west by wagon train. The six events should cover:

   ▣ the first day of the journey (including the reason for traveling west and who is on the journey)
   ▣ the happiest day of the journey (excluding the arrival at the final destination)
   ▣ the saddest day of the journey
   ▣ the hardest day of the journey
   ▣ a major sight or landform seen on the journey
   ▣ the final day of the journey (including the name of the final destination)

CONTINUED ON PAGE 18

2. Next, using the writing strips template, students write a descriptive paragraph to accompany each illustration. Their sentences should be written in the first person, as if the videographer were talking about the illustration as it was being filmed.

3. Hand out copies of the video camera templates (pages 40 and 41). Ask students to cut out and assemble the video cameras. To make the frame sturdier, students can glue the templates to posterboard or oak tag.

4. Ask students to cut out their writing strips, put them in chronological order, and staple them to their video cameras where indicated. Have

them cut out the videotape frames and, following the directions on the template, thread the frames through their cameras. Then have them tape craft sticks to the two ends of the videotape to prevent it from being pulled through the slots.

5. Finally, using the map that they created (see pages 16 and 17), students should write a number along the trail to indicate the place where each segment of their video was taken.

6. Hang the maps and video cameras on a bulletin board under the title "Video Diaries of the Westward Movement."

uilting the Adventure

Materials: copies of page 44, scissors, tape, colored markers or pencils

Quilting was an important job that women performed in the old West, and many quilt patterns were based on the new experiences the early pioneers had on their journey west.

Show some sample quilt patterns to your students. Three are provided at the top of the template on page 44. I like to read *Eight Hands Round: A Patchwork Alphabet* by Ann Whitford Paul (Turtleback Books, 1991) to my class. It shows a different quilt pattern for every letter of the alphabet and discusses how the pattern related to the lives of the early American colonists.

CREATING THE QUILT

1. Have your students think about all of the new sights, landscapes, and landforms the pioneers must have seen. Then ask them to pick an image and think about how they could represent that image geometrically as a quilt pattern.

2. Using the quilt template (page 44), have students draw the geometric shape of the quilt, color the shapes so that they look like pieces of fabric, and cut out the pattern.

3. Then, on the back of the quilt, have students write a paragraph describing the image on the quilt and how it played a role in the lives of the pioneers.

4. Hang the students' quilt patterns side by side on a bulletin board or wall so they form one large quilt. Add a banner that reads "Story Quilts of Our Westward Adventure."

Now & Then Flip Book

Materials: copies of page 45, scissors, colored markers or pencils, white construction paper, glue sticks

Learning about the past helps us to better understand the present, and one way to learn about the past is to contrast the differences between the way people lived back then to the way we live today.

CREATING THE FLIP BOOK

1. Give a copy of the flip book template on page 45 to each student. Have students glue the templates to white construction paper. (This is optional, but it prevents the ink from showing through and gives a more finished look.)

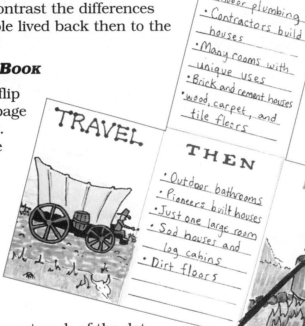

2. Instruct students to cut each of the dotted lines on their templates, making sure to stop where the dotted line meets the solid line. They should fold the flaps down so that the ruled lines are on the inside of the fold, as shown below.

3. Have students place the panels horizontally in front of them so that the flaps lift up. On the cover of each flap, students should use creative lettering to write the title of some aspect of pioneer life that they will contrast with the present (such as travel, cooking, houses, medical care, chores, occupations, the role of women, etc.). They should also draw a picture or icon that represents the topic on which they'll be reporting.

4. On the inside of each flap, students should compare and contrast the way things were in the time of the pioneers with the way things are today. I allow my students to write this information in fragmented sentences and phrases, but you may ask them to pick only one way the topic differs and write two complete paragraphs, one for THEN and one for NOW.

5. Hang the finished flip books on a bulletin board under a banner that reads "My, How Things Have Changed!"

Moving West: Group Project

Materials: will vary depending upon the activities you choose for the groups to do

During your unit on pioneers, you can coordinate a cooperative-group project by using many of the activities in this book that tie into the actual journey west.

COORDINATING THE GROUP PROJECT

1. Divide the class into groups of four or five.

2. Review the requirements of the project with the class (see the list below and on page 21).

3. After the students have completed each component of the project, have them present their information to the class in the form of a group oral report. Invite parents to come watch the presentations. This provides a valuable opportunity for the students to speak in front of groups. It also allows the parents to see what their children have been learning.

4. After the presentations, give each group a large sheet of bulletin board paper (a different color for each group). Ask students to affix all of their projects to the bulletin board paper and write the group members' names on it. Hang the posters in the hall for the whole school to see.

PROJECT REQUIREMENTS LIST

Decide which of the following projects you would like the groups to complete. Stress that part of each group's final grade will be determined by how well each member shares in the production of the final presentation. It will be up to the groups to decide which member(s) will be responsible for completing each element.

Create a Family or Group: Have students create a group of travelers that has as many members as their own group. This can be a family, a group of men traveling to find gold, some slaves who are searching for freedom, or another appropriate group. Ask students to draw a picture of the travelers on a piece of poster board and write the names of the characters under their pictures. When drawing the pictures, students should include things that might appear in the background of the scene. On the back of the poster board, have them list each character, give the vital statistics of the character, and discuss the chores or responsibilities he or she might have had during the journey.

List of Rules: Before a wagon train began its journey, the pioneers needed to decide on a list of rules for the trip. (Some religious groups wouldn't travel on Sundays; some groups with children didn't allow cursing; some said they would leave behind anyone whose wagon axle broke.) Ask each group of students to brainstorm a list of rules to propose to the wagon master. Have them write the list on a piece of construction paper and curl the top and bottom to make it look like a scroll.

Guidebooks: Have each group create a guidebook as described on page 13.

Pioneer Trunks: Ask students to create the pop-up trunks described on pages 14–16. You might also have them make a separate page (or compartment) for each traveler, into which they will pack one luxury item for that person. Underneath the item, they should write a paragraph describing its importance to the owner.

Mapping the Journey: Instruct each group to decide which route their group will take to travel west. Then ask them to create a map on poster board that details the jumping-off point, the trails the group took, and their final destination. Explain that some trails had advantages (such as less snow and flatter terrain), but they also had disadvantages (such as longer distances and hostile natives). Have students mark important sights, stopping points, and landforms that the group might have encountered on their trip. (See the mapping activity on page 16.)

Video Diaries of the Trip West: Ask students to complete the video diary activity on page 17, but have them create nine panels (and mark them on the map they created).

Quilting the Adventure: Make each member of the group responsible for creating a quilt pattern as described on page 18, except have them cut the shapes and patterns out of real cloth scraps (which you can get from a local fabric store). Ask them to glue the shapes onto squares of oak tag and then laminate.

Now & Then Flip Books: Have each group construct two flip books and then tape them together from behind (so that the area where the student will be writing isn't covered by the tape). Ask them to do the brainstorming part of this activity as a group, but then have only one or two group members complete this part of the project.

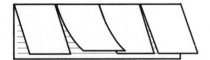

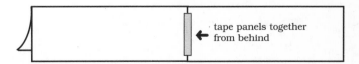

tape panels together
from behind

Gold Fever! – Optimists and Pessimists

Materials: copies of page 46, scissors, lined writing paper, colored markers or pencils

Mining for gold in the days of the gold rush was grueling, dirty work. Many men loved the adventure and the prospect of finding their fortune. Others returned east broke and broken-hearted.

However, life is what you make of it. Many men shared the same experiences, but their different attitudes played an important role in how they saw their adventures.

Auburn Ravine, 1852

CREATING THE SHAPED BOOK

1. Discuss the meaning of the terms *optimist* and *pessimist* with the class.

2. Give students copies of the glass template on page 46. Have them cut it out and use it to trace several other glasses onto lined writing paper.

3. Ask students to cut out these shapes and staple them along the left edge behind the glass to form a book.

4. Invite students to decide whether they want to write about the experience of the California gold rush from an optimistic perspective or a pessimistic one. Have them each write a paragraph in the first person, as if they are one of the men or women who participated in this historic event.

5. When developing their paragraphs, students should consider the following questions:

    - What are your living conditions like during the gold rush?
    - What were your living conditions like before you moved west?
    - Where were you when you first heard about gold being found in California?
    - How did that news make you feel?
    - What is a typical workday like?
    - How do you feel at the end of the day?
    - What are the people you work with like?
    - How do you mine for gold? (Research the various styles of mining.)
    - What tools do you use?

6. On the cover of the glass, the pessimists should write "The Glass Is Half Empty" in the top half of the glass, and the optimists should write "The Glass Is Half Full" in the bottom half of the glass.

7. After students have finished their stories, hang them on a bulletin board under the title "Life Is What You Make of It."

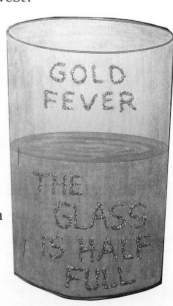

Express Mail

Materials: copies of page 47, envelopes, scissors, colored markers or pencils

Californians felt isolated because they were so far away from the East Coast. It was nearly 2,000 miles from St. Joseph, Missouri, to the west coast of California, and it took months for letters to be delivered by ship, stagecoach, or wagon train. Citizens of Los Angeles, for example, learned that California had been admitted to the Union six weeks after the fact.

CREATING THE SADDLE BAG

1. After reading about the relay system of horse riders called the Pony Express, give each student a copy of the template on page 47.

2. Ask them to color the saddlebag and cut it out, then cut a slit along the dotted line.

3. Have students write a letter from William H. Russell, one of the founders of the Pony Express, seeking backing from potential investors. The letter should include some of the following facts:

   - The Pony Express began on April 3, 1860.
   - On an average day, a rider covered 75–100 miles (of the 2,000-mile journey).
   - Riders changed horses at relay stations, set about 10–15 miles apart.
   - There were approximately 165 relay stations.
   - It took 75 horses to run the route (one way).
   - The Pony Express had about 500 horses and 80 riders.
   - The Pony Express ran day and night, summer and winter.
   - It took mail about 8–10 days to travel across the country in the summer and about 12–16 days in the winter.
   - Riders were paid $100 per month.
   - Horses traveled an average of 10 miles per hour.
   - In the beginning it cost $5 per ½ ounce. By the end of the Pony Express, the service became so popular that the price had dropped to $1 per ½ ounce.

4. After they have written their letters, have students put them in envelopes. Ask them to address their envelopes and create a commemorative stamp showing the cost of delivery.

5. Hang the saddlebags on a bulletin board and put the letters into them. Add a banner that reads "Special Delivery via Pony Express."

Come And Get It! — The Homestead Act

Materials: copies of page 48, scissors, colored markers or pencils

Discuss the Homestead Act and the land rush with your class, and then give each student a copy of the notice template on page 48. (You might show the scene from the movie *Far and Away* that focuses on the land rush.)

CREATING THE ADVERTISEMENT

1. Ask students to use the information they learned to create an advertisement (on the template) meant to entice new farmers to settle the Great Plains area. The advertisement should focus on either the Homestead Act of 1862 or on the land rush, and it should contain related facts. Find examples of old ads and notices on the Internet to give your students a better idea of how they were designed.

2. After they have finished the advertisement, have students cut out the notice.

3. On the back of the notice, ask students to do one of the following:

   ▣ Draw a picture of a farmer in front of his sod house. Write a few sentences describing what it must have been like to live in such a house.
   ▣ Draw a large "╋" on the paper. On the left side, write a list of pros associated with being a homesteader. On the right side, write a list of cons.

4. To display the notices so that both sides can be seen, first tie a string across the length of the classroom about two feet above head level. Next, tie varying lengths of thread from the string. Then tie a paper clip to the ends of the threads. Finally, fasten the notices to the paper clips and allow them to spin freely.

Pioneers Study Guide

Create a wonderful study guide for students by having them compile all of their mini-books, activities, and projects into an interactive pioneers "textbook." Over the course of the unit, ask students to save all of their papers and projects in a pocket folder. At the end of the unit, use a binding machine to put them all together. If you don't have access to one, use a three-hole punch and yarn. Here are suggestions for compiling each page.

Materials: all of the projects students have created, 8½" by 11" paper, glue sticks, binding machine (if available) or hole punch with yarn

COVER

When binding the notebooks, add a page of heavy stock to the front and back. Students can use creative lettering to add a title to their notebook and then draw a total of ten icons around the front and back covers. The icons can represent any ten things students learned over the course of the unit. Ask them to number the icons, and then, on the inside front cover, write a complete sentence describing the significance of each icon.

PAGE 1

Have students glue the MEANDER BOOK OF DANIEL BOONE to the first page. Be sure they include a title. Students may want to add a border or an illustration of Daniel Boone or Kentucky to the page.

PAGE 2

Ask students to turn the POP-UP MONUMENTS page sideways and glue it onto the next page, as shown.

PAGES 3, 4, and 5

Have students use the rough draft of their NATIVE AMERICAN STORY SCROLL as page 3. Ask them to use the copies you made of their groupmates' scrolls as pages 4 and 5.

PAGE 6

The POINT OF VIEW LETTER that expresses the perspective of a pioneer or a Native American can be used for page 6.

PAGE 7

Students can create a pocket-page to hold their TEXAS TIME LINES by folding a piece of 8½" by 11" paper in half horizontally, slipping another sheet of paper into the fold, and taping the sides. Encourage students to add a title and decorate the page.

PAGE 8

Have students glue their GUIDEBOOKS FOR A DIFFICULT JOURNEY onto page 8.

PAGE 9

Have students glue their PIONEER TRUNKS to page 9.

PAGE 10

Page 10 should be the maps students created during the MAPPING THE JOURNEY activity.

PAGE 11

Ask students to create a pocket like they did for page 7 to hold their VIDEO DIARIES. The videotape panels may have to be folded in order for it to fit. Encourage students to add a title and illustration on the pocket.

Take a Video Tour of Our Journey to the Oregon Territory

PAGE 12

Students can create another pocket to hold their QUILTING THE JOURNEY quilt blocks. This makes it easy to remove the quilt block in order to see both sides.

— QUILT BLOCK —
On our journey west we saw the tallest pine trees you could imagine! Papa cut down several dozen and built us a log cabin.

PAGE 13

Have students paste their NOW & THEN FLIP BOOKS onto the next page of their interactive study guides. They should add a title to this page.

Now & Then

PAGE 14

Instruct students to glue the back page of their GLASS-SHAPED BOOKS (which discuss the gold rush) onto page 14 of their study guides.

The California Gold Rush

GOLD FEVER

THE GLASS IS HALF FULL

PAGE 15

Have students use the SADDLEBAG AND PONY EXPRESS LETTERS as the next page.

PAGE 16

Students can create a pocket page to hold their HOMESTEAD ACT NOTICES.

Notice Template

Notice FREE LAND!
First Come, First Served!
You can get 160 acres of FREE LAND at the end of five years if you build a house on it, dig a well, plow 10 acres, fence a section of it, and actually live there. This once-in-a-lifetime offer can be YOURS!

After the interactive study guides are finished, invite your students to have a study-guide sharing day. You may want to display their work on a bulletin board in your classroom or hallway. Remind students to use their study guides when preparing for a test.

Question A—Brainstorming Activity

Ask each of your partners the following question.
Record the person's name and answers in the space provided.

QUESTION A: What are some of the reasons pioneers decided to move west?

RESPONSE #1	RESPONSE #2
_____ (Name)	_____ (Name)

RESPONSE #3	RESPONSE #4
_____ (Name)	_____ (Name)

Question B—Brainstorming Activity

Ask each of your partners the following question.
Record the person's name and answers in the space provided.

QUESTION B: What were some of the difficulties and dangers pioneers faced before and during their journey?

RESPONSE #1	RESPONSE #2
_____ (Name)	_____ (Name)

RESPONSE #3	RESPONSE #4
_____ (Name)	_____ (Name)

Question C—Brainstorming Activity

Ask each of your partners the following question.
Record the person's name and answers in the space provided.

QUESTION C: What methods of transportation did pioneers use?
What differences would they find in today's world?

RESPONSE #1	RESPONSE #2
_____ (Name)	_____ (Name)
Pioneer transportation—	**Pioneer transportation—**
Differences today—	**Differences today—**

RESPONSE #3	RESPONSE #4
_____ (Name)	_____ (Name)
Pioneer transportation —	**Pioneer transportation —**
Differences today—	**Differences today—**

Question D—Brainstorming Activity

Ask each of your partners the following question.
Record the person's name and answers in the space provided.

QUESTION D: What qualities would a pioneer have to possess?

RESPONSE #1

_____
(Name)

_____
_____
_____
_____
_____
_____
_____
_____

RESPONSE #2

_____
(Name)

_____
_____
_____
_____
_____
_____
_____
_____

RESPONSE #3

_____
(Name)

_____
_____
_____
_____
_____
_____
_____

RESPONSE #4

_____
(Name)

_____
_____
_____
_____
_____
_____
_____

Vocabulary Wagon

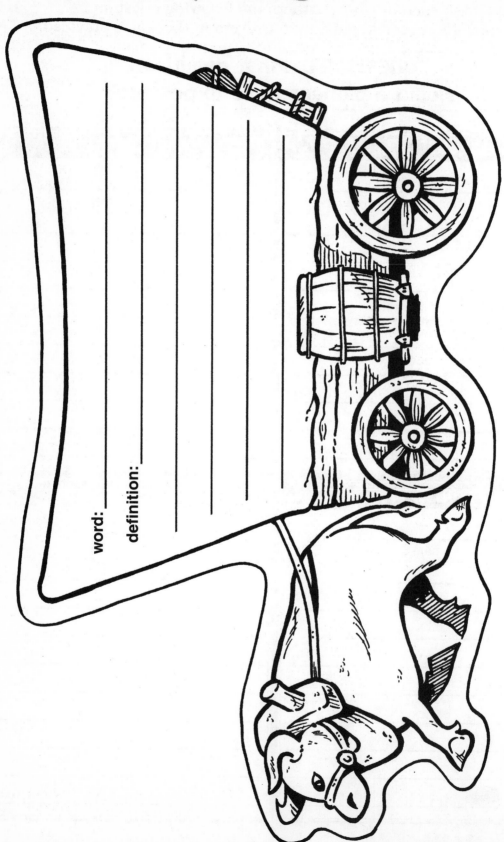

word: _____

definition: _____

① ADVANTAGES AND DISADVANTAGES

List the reasons why people wanted to settle in Kentucky.

List the reasons that the journey to this area was difficult.

---

⑤ **KENTUCKY**

By 1792, enough people were living in Kentucky to make it the fifteenth state. Learn more about Kentucky by finding out the names of the state flower, tree, and bird. Write their names and draw a picture of each in the space provided.

STATE FLOWER

STATE TREE

STATE BIRD

---

③ **WILDERNESS ROAD**

Daniel Boone created the Wilderness Road, a trail that led into Kentucky through the Cumberland Gap.

- Color the Wilderness Road and its symbol in the key red.
- Color the Cumberland Gap and its corresponding symbol green.
- In which state can the Cumberland Gap be found?
- Why is the Cumberland Gap an important landform?

---

⑦ **ADJECTIVES**

Use creative lettering to write six adjectives in the space below that describe Daniel Boone.

Back Cover

② DANIEL BOONE: WOODSMAN

Daniel Boone was once asked if he'd ever been lost.
He replied, "No, but I was bewildered once for three days."
What do you think he meant by this reply?

_____
_____
_____
_____
_____
_____
_____

⑥ nouns

Use creative lettering to write six
nouns in the space below
that describe Daniel Boone.

_____
_____
_____
_____
_____
_____

④ FORT BOONESBORO

Daniel Boone and his men established Fort
Boonesboro in 1778. What were the four
blockhouses at the fort's corners used for?

⑧ DANIEL BOONE: A MINI-BIOGRAPHY

Use the nouns and adjectives from panels 6 and 7
to write a paragraph about Daniel Boone's life.

_____
_____
_____
_____
_____
_____
_____

Map of the Louisiana Purchase

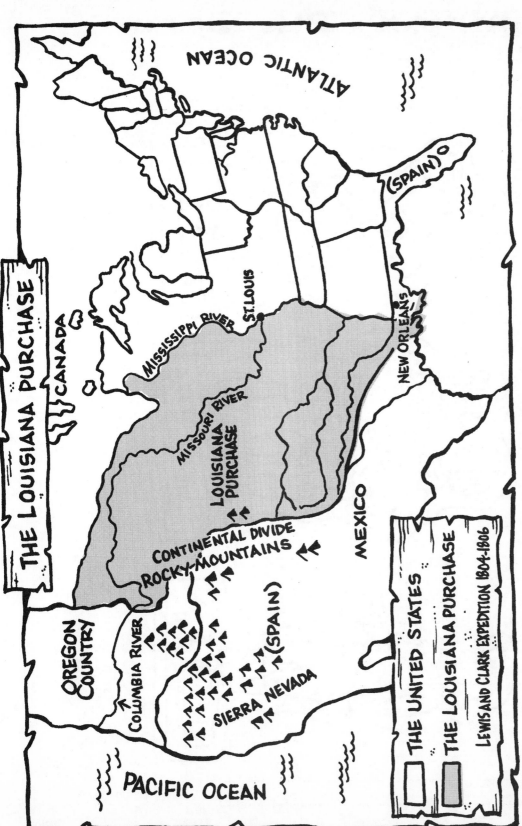

THE LOUISIANA PURCHASE

CANADA

ATLANTIC OCEAN

(SPAIN)

MISSISSIPPI RIVER

ST. LOUIS

MISSOURI RIVER

LOUISIANA PURCHASE

NEW ORLEANS

MEXICO

CONTINENTAL DIVIDE

ROCKY MOUNTAINS

OREGON COUNTRY

COLUMBIA RIVER

(SPAIN)

SIERRA NEVADA

PACIFIC OCEAN

THE UNITED STATES

THE LOUISIANA PURCHASE

LEWIS AND CLARK EXPEDITION 1804-1906

- All of the land to the east of the Mississippi River (except for Florida) belonged to the United States. Color the box in the key and the corresponding U.S. land on the map yellow.
- The land in the central part of the map marked LOUISIANA PURCHASE was the land that the United States purchased from France. Color the box in the key and the corresponding land on the map orange.
- Lewis and Clark's expedition took them from St. Louis up the Missouri River, west along the Columbia River, across the Oregon Country, to the Pacific Ocean. Draw a red line along this route and then make a red line in the key next to the heading for the Lewis and Clark expedition.

Monuments of the Louisiana Purchase

Native American Story Scroll

1821

Mexican Independence

Who ruled the land that is now Texas before 1821?

BEFORE

AFTER

What happened in 1821 to cause this land to change ownership?

(1)

1820s

U.S. Settlers Move to Texas

Describe Stephen Austin's role in the growth of this territory.

How is he honored today?

(2)

1830

Mexico Bans American Settlement of Texas

List five reasons why Mexico banned further settlement of Texas by Americans.

(3)

1836

The Battle for the Alamo / Texas Gains Independence

Describe the importance of each of the following people in Texas's fight for independence.

Antonio López de Santa Anna

William Travis

Jim Bowie

(4)

Juan Seguín

Davy Crockett

(5)

Sam Houston

1845

Texas Admitted to the Union

It took a long time before the U.S. allowed Texas into the Union. List two reasons for this resistance.

(6)

(7)

Trails to the West

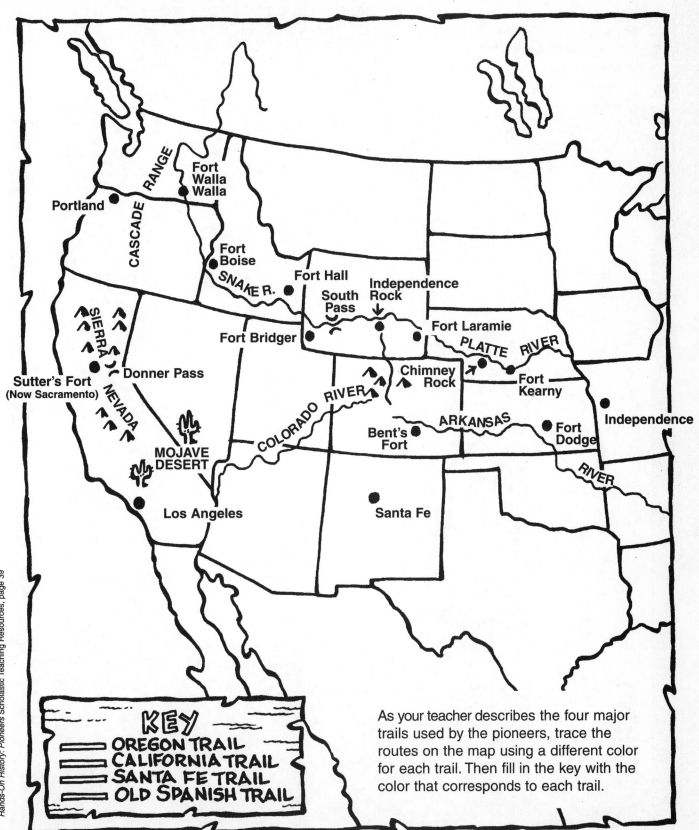

KEY
- OREGON TRAIL
- CALIFORNIA TRAIL
- SANTA FE TRAIL
- OLD SPANISH TRAIL

As your teacher describes the four major trails used by the pioneers, trace the routes on the map using a different color for each trail. Then fill in the key with the color that corresponds to each trail.

Map labels:
CASCADE RANGE, Fort Walla Walla, Portland, Fort Boise, SNAKE R., Fort Hall, Independence Rock, South Pass, SIERRA, Fort Bridger, Donner Pass, Fort Laramie, PLATTE RIVER, NEVADA, Sutter's Fort (Now Sacramento), Chimney Rock, Fort Kearny, COLORADO RIVER, MOJAVE DESERT, Bent's Fort, ARKANSAS, Fort Dodge, Independence, RIVER, Los Angeles, Santa Fe

ideo Camera Cover

1. Glue the video camera cover to a sheet of poster board and cut it out.
2. Write your name and the title of your report in the rectangle at the top of the video camera. Use creative lettering.

Title:

Video Camera Interior

1. Glue the video camera interior to a sheet of poster board and cut it out.
2. Tape the left edge of the cover to the left edge of the interior so it opens like a book.

Slot B

Cut slots A and B. Thread your film through slot A from behind and through slot B so only one frame can be seen at a time. Then tape each end tab around a craft stick to prevent it from being pulled through.

Slot A

Place writing sheets here.

Put your writing sheets in order and staple the left edges so they cover these instructions.

Film Strips

After you thread your videotape through the camera, glue this tab to a craft stick.

After you thread your videotape through the camera, glue this tab to a craft stick.

Glue this tab behind panel 3.

Writing Strips

Panel #   :

Panel #   :

Panel #   :

Panel #   :

Quilt Pattern Template

These three quilt patterns are called (from left to right) Log Cabin, Maple Leaf, and Honeycomb.

NOW | THEN

NOW | THEN

NOW | THEN

NOW | THEN

Glass Template

Saddlebag Template

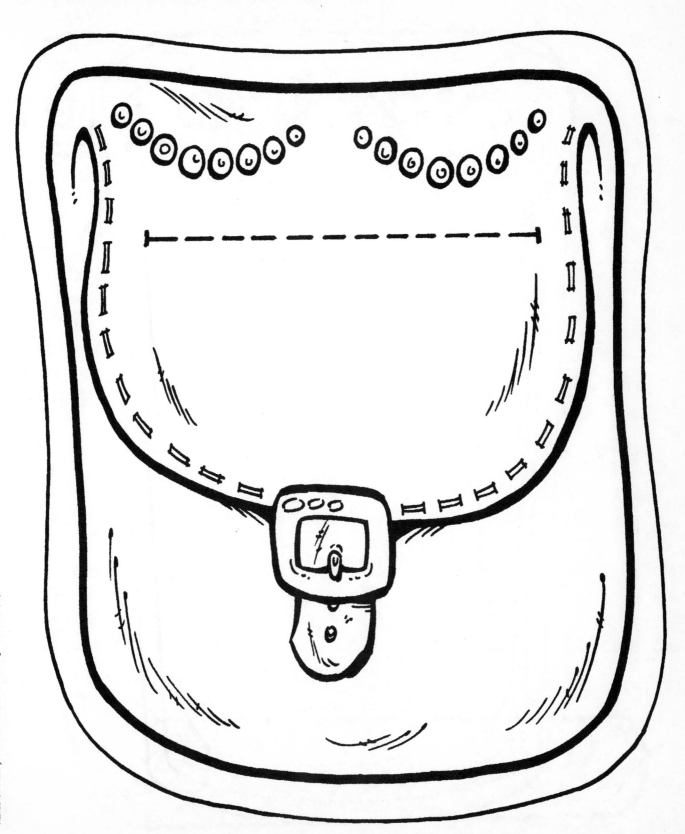

Notice Template